the extraordinary book that invents itself

Written by
Alison Buxton and Helen Bell,
STEAMWORKS

Illustrated by Pintachan

CUT OUT and MAKE the PROJECTS. SAVE the INSTRUCTION STRIPS for your INVENTOR'S HANDBOOK.

EARTHAWARE
KIDS

A message from Alison Buxton and Helen Bell, the inventors of STEAMWORKS

Hey there budding inventor!

Wherever you are reading these words, look around you. We're sure you'll see many inventions that help you every day, from microwaves and marker pens, to tin cans and toilet paper.

Incredible inventions are happening all the time, often because somebody, somewhere is trying to solve a problem.

What's the best way to recycle plastic?

How do we get to Mars?

Can we make cars fly?

But inventions don't always have to be big, and inventors aren't always adults. Did you know that ear muffs, trampolines, and toy trucks were invented by children?

In this book, we've chosen some of our **favorite inventions** to look at in closer detail. You will not only learn about inventions like **code-breaking, bionic hands, and rockets**, but you can also **use the pages of this extraordinary book to recreate them!** To help you along, we've designed some templates. Think of these as **frameworks to guide you.** Each colorful template will show you where to cut out, fold, stick, or tape.

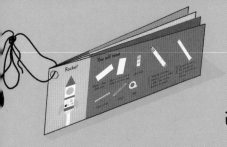

As you complete each project, **tear off the instruction strips** at the bottom of the page. Thread them together and you'll have your very own **inventor's handbook** to keep and use again.

Great inventors always have their most **useful tools at the ready.** Scissors, tape, and glue will come in very handy as you move through this book. At times, you may need some extra bits and pieces, so always **check the You will need section** before you start.

At the end of each project, you'll see a box marked **What next?** You could say that this is the most important stage of all. Use this step to go wild and take the invention to another level. **Tinker, trial, and test.** Your experimenting may spark an idea that leads to a brand-new amazing invention!

Good luck and happy inventing!

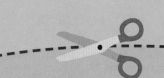

Alison and Helen invented a company called **STEAMWORKS.** By setting up workshops and working with schools, **STEAMWORKS** is on a mission to inspire future inventors, engineers, scientists, makers, and digital masterminds.

Helen
Bell

Alison
Buxton

CONTENTS

EXPLORE ROBOTICS
by making a bionic hand

1

Cut out and make a moving robot hand.

Robotic hands are designed to mimic, or copy, the movements of human hands. They grasp, lift, carry, and move objects.

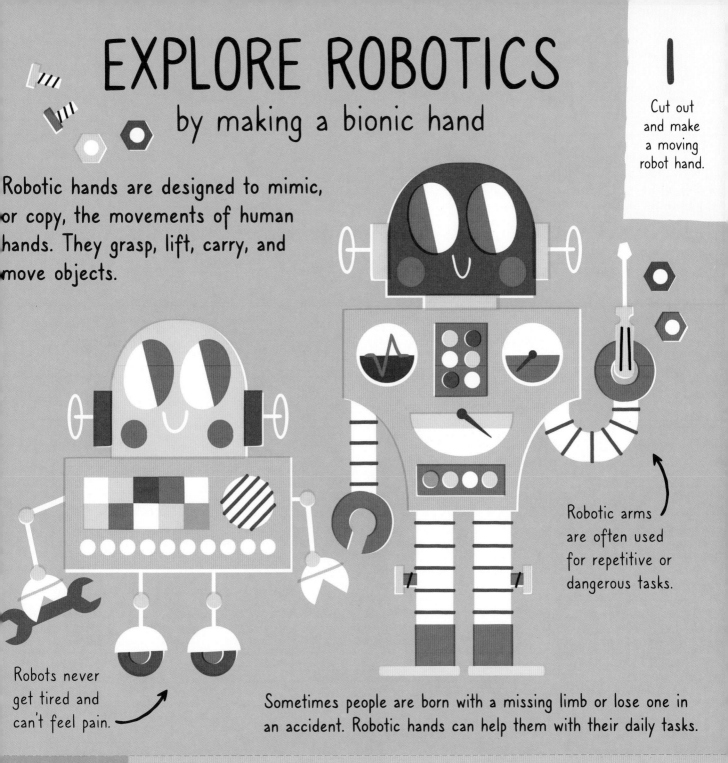

Robotic arms are often used for repetitive or dangerous tasks.

Robots never get tired and can't feel pain.

Sometimes people are born with a missing limb or lose one in an accident. Robotic hands can help them with their daily tasks.

Robotic hand

You will need

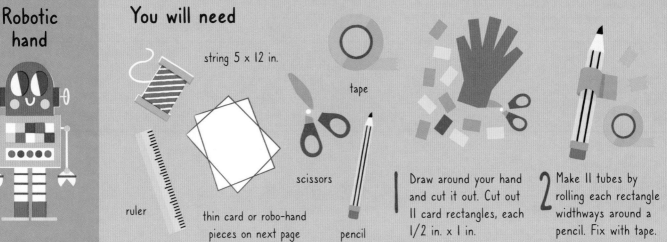

string 5 x 12 in.

tape

ruler

thin card or robo-hand pieces on next page

scissors

pencil

1 Draw around your hand and cut it out. Cut out 11 card rectangles, each 1/2 in. x 1 in.

2 Make 11 tubes by rolling each rectangle widthways around a pencil. Fix with tape.

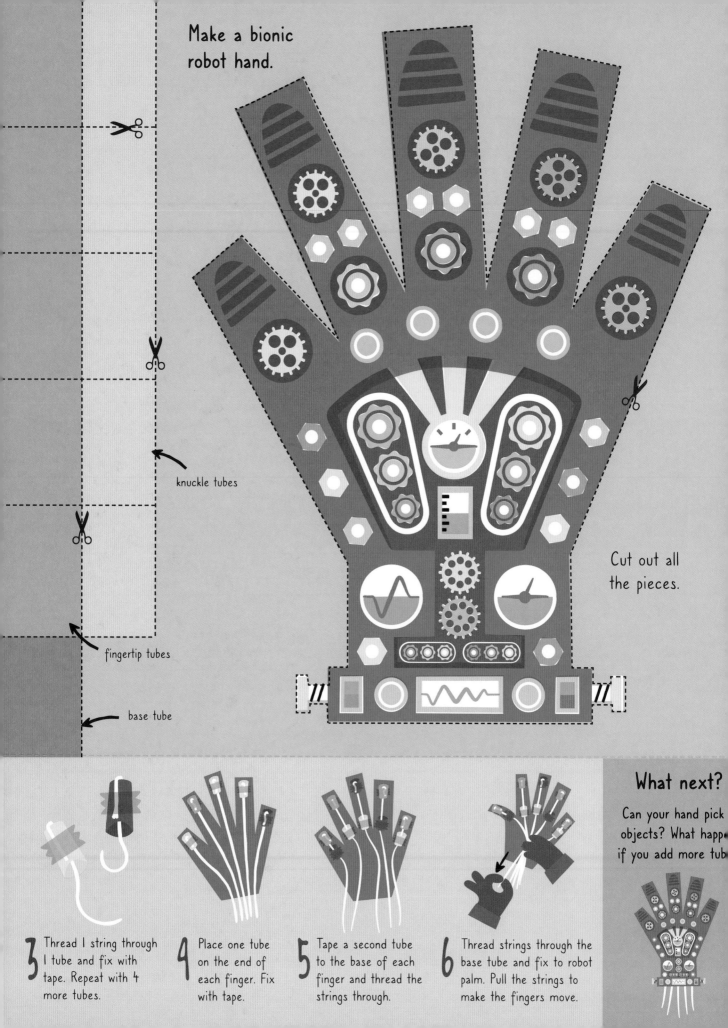

Make a bionic robot hand.

knuckle tubes

fingertip tubes

base tube

Cut out all the pieces.

3 Thread 1 string through 1 tube and fix with tape. Repeat with 4 more tubes.

4 Place one tube on the end of each finger. Fix with tape.

5 Tape a second tube to the base of each finger and thread the strings through.

6 Thread strings through the base tube and fix to robot palm. Pull the strings to make the fingers move.

What next?

Can your hand pick objects? What happe if you add more tub

STUDY THE STARS
with a constellation viewer

2 Make a viewer to recognize star patterns.

Star constellations are patterns of stars in the night sky. Telescopes were invented to take a closer look at these stars.

Ursa Minor
(Little Bear)

Pegasus the Horse

Draco the Dragon

A telescope's lens magnifies the light from the stars, making them appear closer.

Since ancient times, sailors have used the positions of the stars to help them find their way at sea.

Constellation viewer

You will need

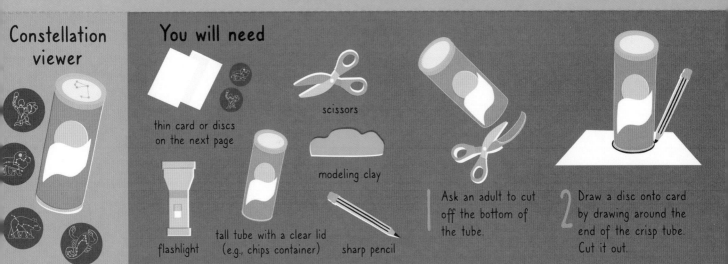

thin card or discs on the next page

scissors

modeling clay

flashlight

tall tube with a clear lid (e.g., chips container)

sharp pencil

Ask an adult to cut off the bottom of the tube.

2 Draw a disc onto card by drawing around the end of the crisp tube. Cut it out.

Orion

Orion is a famous hunter in ancient Greek legend.

Press out the star gazer discs to make constellations on your bedroom wall.

Scorpio

Tucana

Can you see the shape of a scorpion?

Tucana is named after the toucan.

Leo

Which African animal can you see?

Why do you think Ursa Major is nicknamed the Great Bear?

Ursa Major

What next?

Use your viewer to learn the star patterns, and look for them in the night sky.

3 Draw the stars of your favorite constellation onto the card disc.

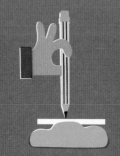

4 Make holes for each star with a pencil. Protect the surface with modeling clay.

5 Push the disc into the tube lid and put the lid on.

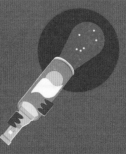

6 Turn the flashlight on and the lights out. Point your stargazer onto an empty wall.

WATCH ANIMALS
to spark an idea

3

Make a leaping frog to trigger new ideas.

Some inventors look at animals for inspiration. This is called biomimicry. Frogs have sparked many discoveries!

Designers looked at the frog's webbed feet while inventing flippers for swimming.

A frog's super-grippy feet inspired inventors to make nonslip car tires.

Robot scientists are interested in how frogs move in wet, slimy mud. They are inventing tiny robots to move inside our bodies and help us when we're ill.

Leaping frog

You will need

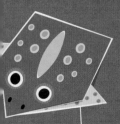

card 5 in. x 8 in. or template on next page

1 Cut out a piece of card. Fold the top corner down to line up with the edge, then open. Do the same to the other side.

2 Bring the top fold down while gently pushing the side flaps inward. Press down firmly.

Fold a frog and make it leap!

Fold along the white dotted lines.

✂

What next?

Look at the way animals move. Can you spot something that might just lead to the next big invention?

3 Turn the bottom points of the triangles up to make the front legs.

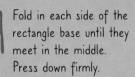

4 Fold in each side of the rectangle base until they meet in the middle. Press down firmly.

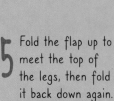

5 Fold the flap up to meet the top of the legs, then fold it back down again.

6 Turn it over. Hold your finger at the bottom of the frog. Pull your finger off and watch it leap!

INVESTIGATE BALANCE
to find the center of gravity

4
Make a balancing acrobat.

The ancient Egyptians invented balance scales. They help us to measure how heavy objects are.

The center of gravity is the point where the weight is evenly spread and all sides are in balance.

Ancient Egyptians believed the gods weighed their hearts to enter the afterlife.

When the pans are balanced, the weight of objects is equal.

Balancing acrobat

You will need

pencil

thin card or acrobats on the next page

paper clips

GLUE

glue stick

scissors

1 Draw a symmetrical acrobat, with long arms, doing a handstand.

2 Cut out your acrobat. Color it in if you'd like to.

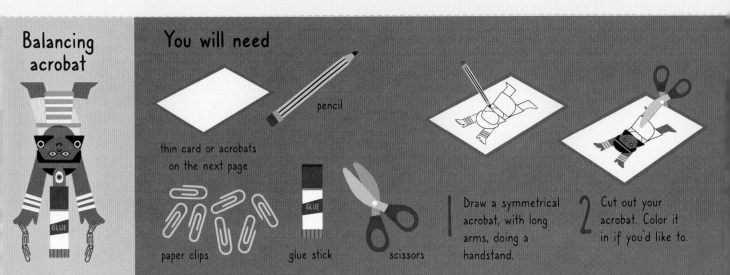

Cut out these templates to make some balancing toys.

Try balancing your acrobats on a taut (stretched) piece of string or wool.

balancing point

position of paper clips

3 Add three or four paper clips to each arm so they dangle down.

4 Try to balance the acrobat on a glue stick. You may need to add more paper clips.

How does it work?

Normally, when we try to balance a thin object, it tips over.

By adding the paper clips to the bottom of the arms, we move the center of gravity below the balancing point, allowing it to balance more easily.

What next?

Try inventing your own balancing toy.

BUILD A BRIDGE
using strong shapes

Bridges were invented so that people could travel across rivers, lakes, and valleys. They are made from strong shapes like triangles and arches.

Arches help to spread the load so they can carry more weight.

Truss bridge

You will need

10 x card strips 8 in. x 1 in. or pieces on the next page

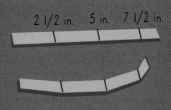

2 1/2 in.   5 in.   7 1/2 in.

pencil   glue   1 card rectangle 8 in. x 2 in. or template

1 Mark each thin strip at 2 1/2 in., 5 in., and 7 1/2 in. Fold along the lines.

2 Fold each strip into a triangle by gluing the small flap.

Use these pieces
to make a strong
triangular bridge.

Remember!
Triangles are quite a
strong shape, but if w•
connect lots of triangle
together, we can make
them super strong.

What next?

Make more triangles
make an even stron
bridge. How strong c
you make your bridg

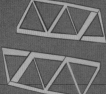

3 Glue five triangles
together in a row.
Repeat with the other
five to form two beams.

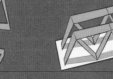

4 Glue both beams to
the card rectangle.

5 Turn your model
over. You have a
truss bridge!

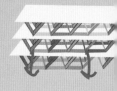

6 How much weight can
your bridge take? Test
it out with different
toys and objects.

CREATE A TV SHOW
to entertain your friends

The first TV shows were black and white.

What's your favorite TV show?

Today, we watch TV programs on computers, phones, and televisions. But one hundred years ago, TV hadn't even been invented.

Hand-powered television

You will need

small cardboard box approx 6 in. wide and 12 in. long

2 cardboard paper towel tubes

ruler

pens

8 in. x 11-in. paper

tape

scissors

1 Draw around the tubes 1/2 in. from the top and bottom edges of the side of the box.

2 Repeat on the other side and cut all the circles out. Push the tubes through.

This is an alien story told in pictures. Will your TV story be about aliens? Or perhaps you prefer wizard, unicorn, or detective tales.

Turn the rolls to tell your story.

3 Draw 1/2 in. around the edge of the front of the box and ask an adult to help you cut it out.

4 Cut the A4 paper in half lengthwise. Tape the two strips together to make one long strip.

5 Draw squares down the paper and fill in the boxes with pictures that tell a story.

6 Tape the top of the strip to the top roller. Turn the roll to wind the paper up. Tape the bottom to the bottom roll.

What next?

Make sound effects to go with your TV story. Use more paper to make a longer story roll.

TEST STRENGTH
by weaving threads

Baskets can be made from grasses, straw, trees, and vines. When they are woven together, they are super strong.

Bendy branches are threaded in and out to make a super-strong willow basket.

Basket

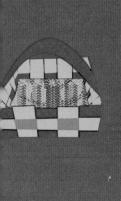

You will need

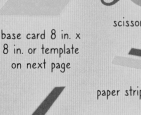

scissors

pencil

base card 8 in. x 8 in. or template on next page

paper strips 1/2 in. deep

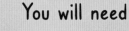

paper handle 8 in. x 1 in.

ruler

glue

1 Measure 2 in. from each corner of the base card. Draw lines to connect them into a square. Cut off the corners.

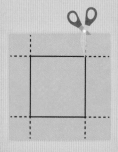

2 Draw lines every 3/4 in. from the edge on each of the flaps. Cut along these lines.

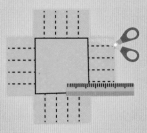

Fold along the dotted white lines.

Use this template to make your own basket.

What next?

Try using wool, string and thread instead of paper. Which is the strongest?

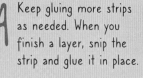

3 Fold up the flaps. Glue a paper strip to the base of one of the flaps. Weave it in and out.

4 Keep gluing more strips as needed. When you finish a layer, snip the strip and glue it in place.

5 Weave 3 layers. Fold the little flaps inwards and fix in place with glue.

6 Glue the paper handle to each basket edge.

DESIGN A GLIDER
to swoop through the air

Gliders are light aircraft that fly without needing an engine. To get into the air, they need a tow from an airplane and are then released.

Lift

Drag

Drag slows the glider down.

Lift is the force that keeps the glider in the air. Lift is mostly provided by the wings.

Thrust is the force that propels aircraft into the air. When you throw a glider, your arm provides the thrust.

Ring glider

You will need

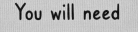

3 x card strips 1 in. x 5 in. or strips on next page

tape

straw

1 Join the ends of one card strip into a loop and tape to secure.

2 Tape the other two strips together and glue the ends to make a large loop.

tape

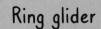

Make a ring glider.

Ring-shaped glider wings reduce drag. The curved ring shape is more aerodynamic and will help the glider to fly further.

Use these templates to make a simple ring glider.

Use these strips to make more loops.

What next?

Tinker by adding more and fewer loops to your glider.

What happens to the way it flies?

Cut the straw to 5 in. long.

Tape a loop to each end. Make sure the loops line up nice and straight.

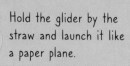

Hold the glider by the straw and launch it like a paper plane.

BREAK THE CODE
to reveal a message

9
Make a code wheel to send a secret note.

Spies use codes to send and receive top secret information. To crack a code and reveal a hidden message, you need to look for patterns.

Computers use a special language called binary code to send instructions to each other.

Binary code uses only 1 and 0, so it is difficult to crack.

Code breaker

CODE	
A • T	C • N
B • G	F • O
C • S	J • P
D • A	W • Q
E • U	D • R
F • B	Z • S
G • P	L • T
H • Q	M • U
I • N	H • V
J • Y	E • W
K • X	J • X
L • R	O • Y
M • K	I • Z
MAKER	

You will need

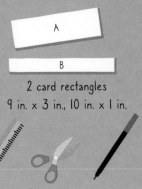

2 card rectangles
9 in. x 3 in., 10 in. x 1 in.

ruler   scissors   pen

1 Measure 1/2 in. up from the long edge of card A. Starting at 1 in., mark a dot every 1/2 in. until you have 15 dots. Repeat along the top edge.

2 Draw a line between the first two dots and the last two dots. Ask an adult to snip along these lines to make slits.

Make a code wheel

1 Cut out the circles and ask an adult to make a hole in the center of each.

2 Put the small wheel on top of the large wheel and line up the holes. Join together with a paper fastener.

3 Turn the wheel to set the code.

Write a secret note using the symbols.

Tell a friend where to set the code wheel so they can decipher the message.

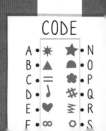

---

3 Write A–M down one side along the dots, and N–Z down the other.

A •	• N
B •	• O
C •	• P
D •	• Q
E •	• R
F •	• S
G •	• T
H •	• U
I •	• V
J •	• W
K •	• X
L •	• Y
M •	• Z

4 Slip the thin card through the slits. Add each alphabet letter randomly against a dot.

CODE

A • T	C • N
B • G	F • O
C • S	J • P
D • A	W • Q
E • U	D • R
F • B	Z • S
G • P	L • T
H • Q	M • U
I • N	H • V
J • Y	E • W
K • X	J • X
L • R	O • Y
M • K	I • Z

MAKER

5 Write a message by finding each letter and using the one next to it instead.

CODE

A • T	C • N
B • G	F • O
C • S	J • P
D • A	W • Q
E • U	D • R
F • B	Z • S
G • P	L • T
H • Q	M • U

QURRF!

MAKER

6 Make an identical strip for a friend so they can read your coded messages.

What next?

Make a strip with symbols on it instead of letters.

CODE

A ☀ ★	N
B ▲ ♥	O
C ≡ ♣	P
D ♪ ✳	Q
E ♥ ☰	R
F ∞ ○	S

USE SHADOWS
to measure time

Have you noticed how your shadows are longer or shorter at different times of the day? The ancient Egyptians used this idea to invent the earliest type of clock—a sundial.

As the sun moves higher in the sky toward the middle of the day, your shadow gets shorter.

As the Earth spins, the sun's position in the sky changes gradually throughout the day.

When the sun is low in the sky, late in the day, your shadow is very long.

Sundial

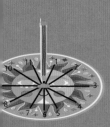

You will need

card or template on the next page

scissors

plate to draw around

sticky tack

ruler

pencil

outdoor space

sunny day

1 Draw a circle on the card. You could draw around a small plate. Cut it out carefully.

2 Draw a straight line from the center of the circle to the edge. Write the number 12.

Use this template to make a sundial.

12

HANDY TIP!
Tape your sundial onto a garden table so that it won't move out of place.

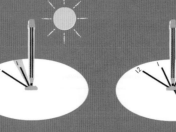

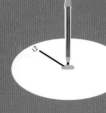

3 Attach sticky tack to the centre. Use this to hold an upright pencil in place.

4 Put your sundial outside in the sun at 12 noon. Line up the pencil's shadow with the 12.

5 Leave outside for 1 hour. At 1 o'clock, draw a line along the new shadow and write 1 at the edge.

6 Draw a line and number it every hour until the sun sets. This will create your dial.

What next?

On the next sunny day, try to tell the time on your sundial by looking at where the shadow is lying.

EXPLORE SOUND
with a harmonica

11

Make music with a homemade harmonica.

Sounds are made when objects vibrate. The vibrations enter your ear and you hear different sounds. This is how musical instruments work.

tuba

trumpet

When you blow into a harmonica, reeds inside vibrate to make sound.

double bass

harmonica

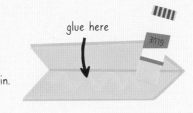

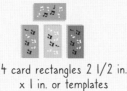

Harmonica

You will need

2 card rectangles 6 in. x 2 1/2 in. or pieces on next page

4 card rectangles 2 1/2 in. x 1 in. or templates

glue here

paper strip 6 in. x 1 in.

glue stick

tape

scissors

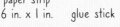

1 Cut out the card pieces. Fold the large rectangles of card lengthwise and glue.

2 Roll each small rectangle around a pencil and tape in place. Squash each tube a little.

Use these templates to make your very own harmonica.

Fold along the white dotted lines.

Your harmonica makes its sound when you blow on the thin paper strip, causing it to vibrate.

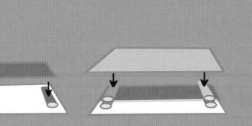

3 Cut out the strip of paper

4 Glue 2 tubes to each end of one folded card. Glue the top of the tubes. Fix the paper strip on top.

5 Glue 2 tubes onto each end of the paper strip. Glue tops of the tubes. Press on second card.

6 Hold your harmonica at each end and blow through the middle.

What next?

Can you change the pitch of your harmonica by blowing harder or softer?

Invent another instrument using recycled material

USE A PULLEY
to lift a heavy weight

12
Build your own powerful pulley.

Pulleys are simple machines that help us to lift or move objects with less effort.

This pulley is attached to a zip wire. It lets you zoom from tree to tree.

Pulley

You will need

2 x card discs (3-in. diameter)

Strip of card (approx. 8 in. x 1 in.)

string

scissors

sharp pencil

a basket or toy

glue

modelling clay

strong tape

ruler

1 Draw 2 lines 1/2 in. deep across the strip. Fold them in slightly.

2 Draw lines 1/2 in. apart on both sides. Snip each up to the line.

Use these templates to make your own pulleys.

3 Glue one end, fold into a circle, and attach to the other end.

4 Attach a disk to each side by gluing the tops of the little flaps.

5 Press a pencil through the center of the wheel. Use modeling clay to protect the surface.

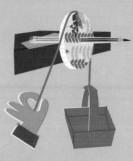

6 Tape the pulley to a table. Tie a toy to a piece of string. Loop it over and pull!

What next?

Add more pulley wheels. More whee[...] mean even less eff[...]

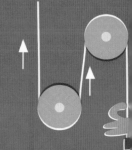

CONJURE UP MAGIC
by walking through paper

Magicians invent magic tricks to entertain and amaze a crowd. Tricks and illusions make seemingly impossible events appear real.

Magicians practice their tricks lots of times so that no one can see how they are done.

The key to a great trick is in the presentation.

Magic trick

You will need

card or paper
7 in. x 7 in.
or template

pencil

ruler

scissors

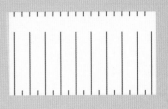

1 Fold the card in half. Mark every 1/2 in. along the top and bottom of the folded card.

2 Starting at the folded side, draw a 3-in. line up from the first mark. Repeat along every other mark.

Use this template to perfom the impossible paper trick.

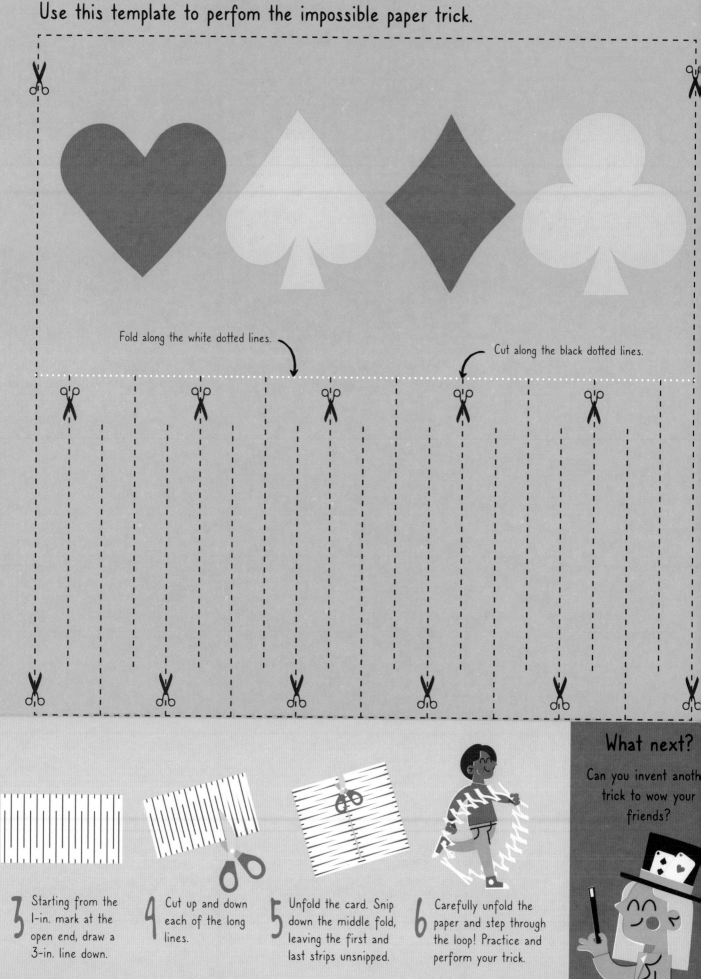

Fold along the white dotted lines.

Cut along the black dotted lines.

3 Starting from the 1-in. mark at the open end, draw a 3-in. line down.

4 Cut up and down each of the long lines.

5 Unfold the card. Snip down the middle fold, leaving the first and last strips unsnipped.

6 Carefully unfold the paper and step through the loop! Practice and perform your trick.

What next?

Can you invent anoth[er] trick to wow your friends?

LOOK AT NATURE
for creative ideas

Inventors often use ideas from nature to spark their imagination. How do you think these spinning seeds helped engineers to design helicopters and drones?

The spinning slows the seed's fall so it can travel far away.

Maple trees have winged seeds that spin as they fall.

Try making your own spinning helicopter.

Helicopter

You will need

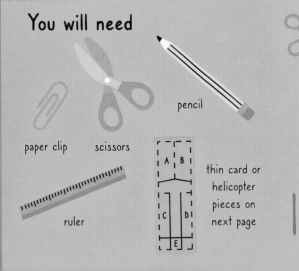

paper clip   scissors   pencil

ruler

thin card or helicopter pieces on next page

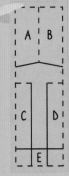

1 Cut out or copy the pieces on the next page or the inside back cover.

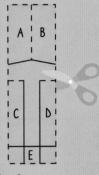

2 Cut along the black dotted lines.

The super-fast, spinning blades keep the helicopter up in the air.

A

B

Fold along the white dotted lines.

C

D

E

What next?

Try different sizes. Let them drop from a high window. Which travels the furthest?

3 Fold A along the line toward you and B away from you.

4 Fold C & D into the middle.

5 Fold E upward and secure in place with a paper clip.

USE NATURE'S POWER
by harnessing the wind

Wind turbines turn the movement of the wind into electrical power. The shape of the blades or sails catch the wind, and this pushes them around.

When lots of wind turbines are built in the same area, it is known as a wind farm.

Try making your own wind catcher.

Spinning windmill

You will need

thin card 7 in. x 7 in. or windmill template on next page

hole punch

paper fastener   scissors

paper straw

1 Fold the paper diagonally both ways. While folded, punch a hole in the center of the square.

2 Open the square and cut just over halfway along each fold line.

Try using this template to make a windmill.

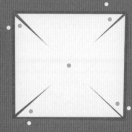

3 Punch four holes as shown—one in each triangle.

Keep this!

4 Cut 1/4 in. off the end of the straw. Flatten one end and punch a hole.

5 Fold each outer hole to meet the center hole and secure with a paper fastener.

6 Thread on the 1/4 in. piece of straw. Add the large straw and open the paper fastener.

What next?

Make more and crea[...]
your own wind farm

DESIGN A POSTCARD

using a print block

16

Print your own cards with a potato.

Before printers were invented, everything had to be hand-drawn and handwritten. Printing machines allowed books and posters to be made in large numbers.

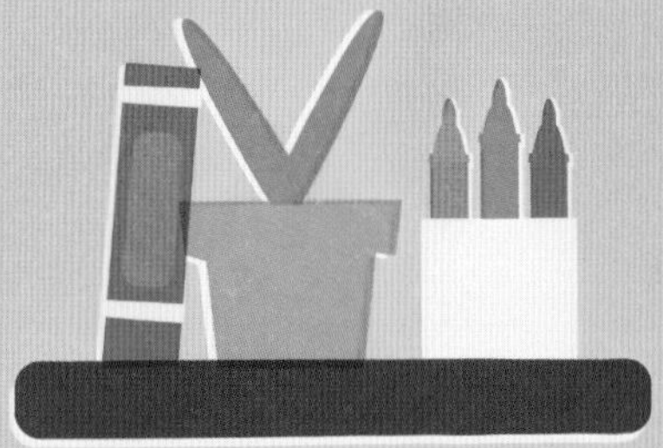

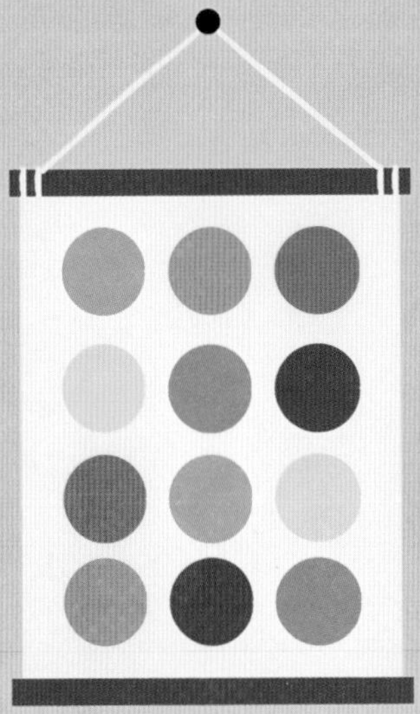

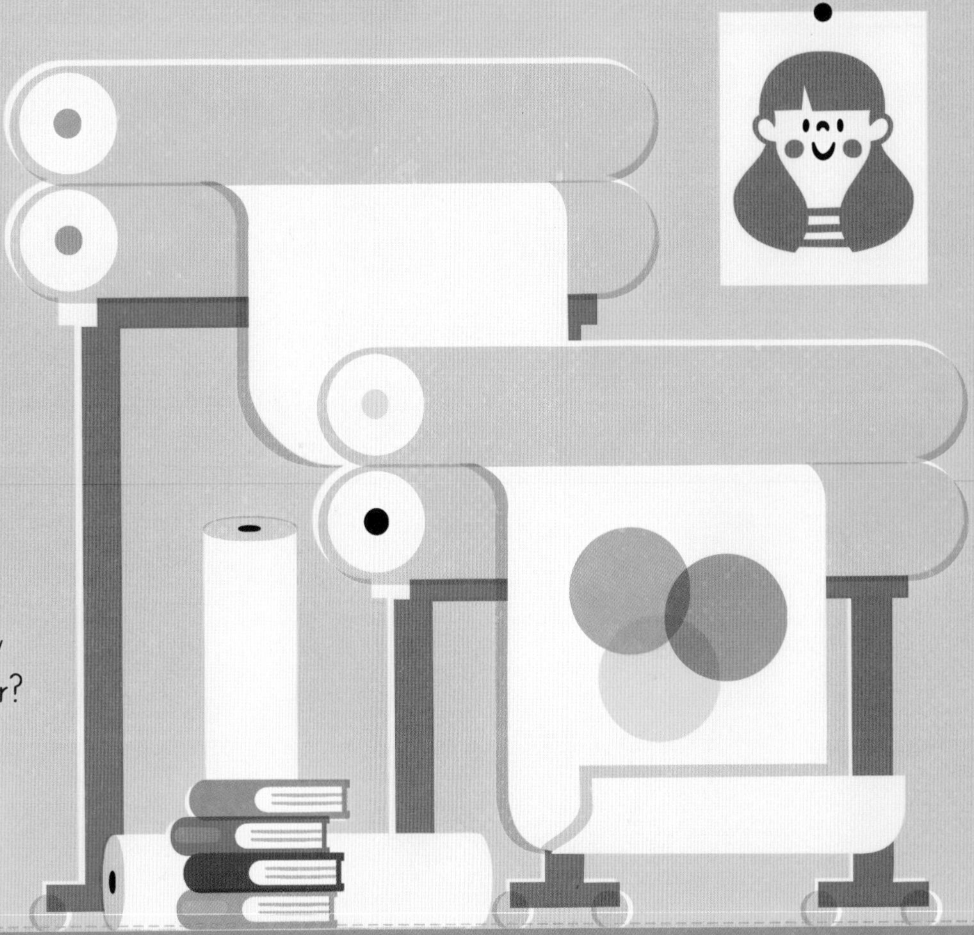

You can print the same picture again and again very quickly. Do you use a printer?

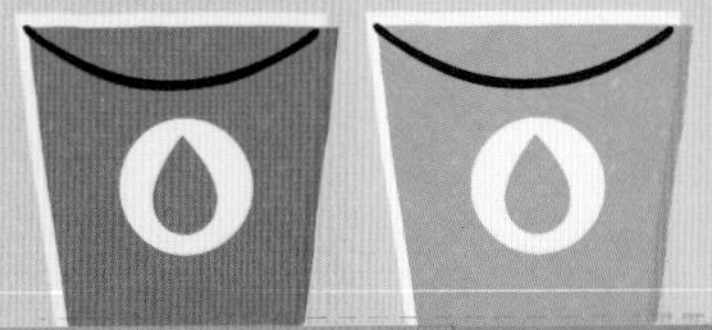

Potato prints

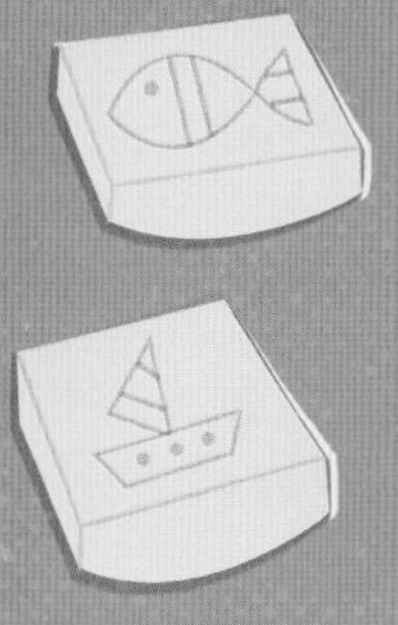

You will need

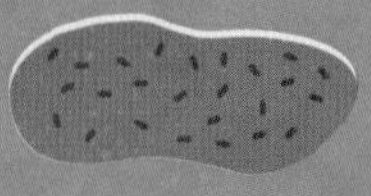

potato

card

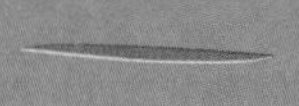

cocktail stick

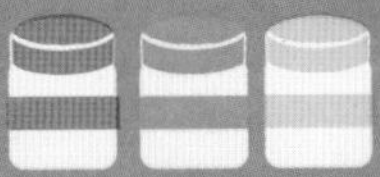

poster paint

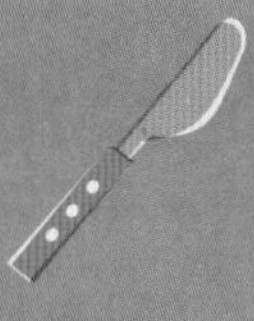

knife

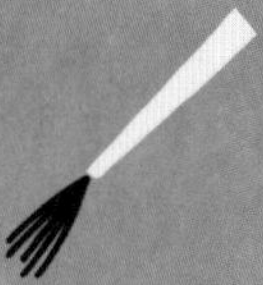

paintbrush

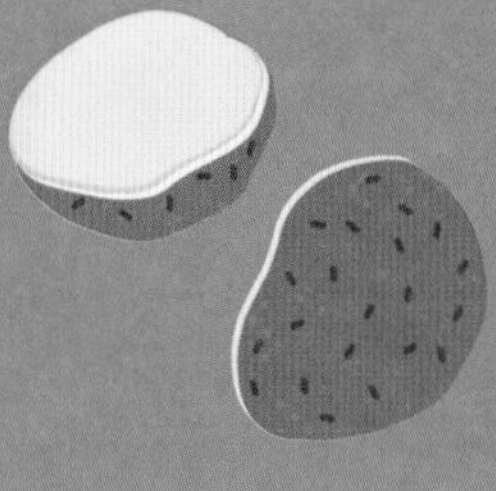

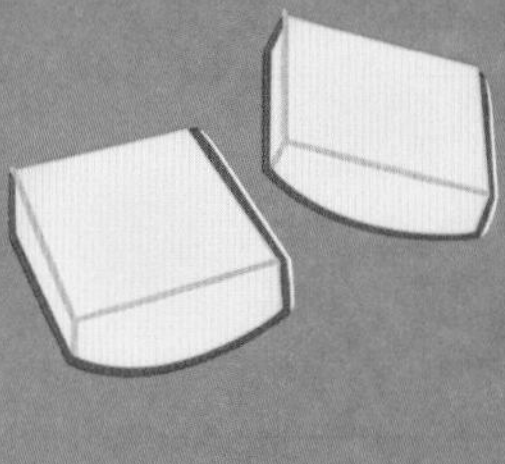

1 Ask an adult to cut the potato in half with a knife.

2 The edges need to be cut off to make two flat rectangles.

Try printing with these shapes. Cut out a handle, fold it in half, and stick half to the shape so you can hold it.

Fold along the white dotted lines

glue

glue

glue

What next?

Make prints with card shapes. Use the templates above, or make your own!

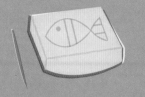

3 Use the cocktail stick to mark a pattern on the cut side of the potato.

4 Paint the surface of the potato with thick poster paint.

5 Print your design on the postcard. When it is dry, you can write a message and post it to a friend.

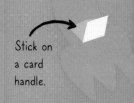

Stick on a card handle.

DISCOVER MECHANICS
by making a grabber arm

Mechanics is about understanding how things move. Robot arms work like ours and can do lots of useful jobs for us.

Grabber arms have joints, just like our elbows and fingers, that help them to bend, stretch, and grip.

Grabber arm

You will need

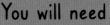

6 card strips
8 in. x 1 in. or templates

card or templates

hole punch

glue stick

7 paper fasteners

scissors

1 Cut out the card strips. Fold each strip of card in half and glue them firmly together.

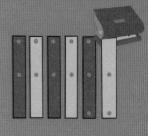

2 Make a hole in the center and at the end of each strip. On two strips, make a hole at the other end too.

handles

teeth

What next?

Can you make a longer grabber? How do you make it turn corners?

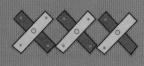

3 Connect the strips with paper fasteners. Make sure the two strips with the three holes are together.

4 Connect the X shapes to each other with paper fasteners, as shown.

5 Cut out 2 handle shapes, as shown. Fold in half, stick together with glue, and attach to one end of the grabber.

6 Cut out the two ovals, fold in half, and stick together with glue. Snip teeth and attach to the other ends.

MAKE MOVING PICTURES
with an optical illusion

When you watch a cartoon, you are seeing lots of pictures put together, one after another. Played at high speed, the pictures trick your brain into thinking they are moving.

It takes 24 pictures of the cowboy to make one second of animated film!

Spinning picture

You will need

thin card or templates

pens

jar lid

scissors

straw

glue

1 Use a jar lid to draw two circles on card. Cut them out.

2 Draw a picture on each card circle. They will combine into one image.

WANTED

Try out these templates.

What next?

Make up your own design. Does black white work better than color?

Glue the back of one disk and press a straw into the middle.

Glue the back of the other disk. Press the disks together with the straw in the center.

Hold the straw between your hands and spin it back and forth. Do the pictures merge together?

DESIGN A BOAT
to carry cargo

nventors have to work hard to keep
a boat afloat. It's not always about
the size—it's also about the
weight and shape.

Shape—a large, flat shape will float
more easily than a tall, narrow shape.

Make your own boat by
tinkering around with the
shape of the hull.

Weight—if the hull, or body, of a ship is full of air,
the boat is much lighter in the water, so it floats.

Model boat

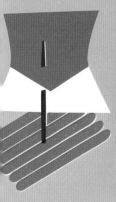

You will need

toothpicks

card or pieces on
the next page

old boxes and scrap
materials, corks, avocado
skins, sponge, cartons

rubber
bands

modeling clay

string

tape

scissors

sticks

Cork boat

Attach 3 corks together
with a rubber band. Stick
a toothpick in the middle
cork and add a card flag.

Avocado boat

Wash out half an avocado
skin. Stick some modeling
clay in the bottom to hold
a toothpick mast.

Try out these sails, funnels, and flags on your model boats.

Funnel

Sails

Flags

Stick boat

Tie some sticks together with string. Use a ball of modeling clay to attach a toothpick mast and a flag.

Tub boat

Wash a used food tub. Roll up a piece of card 7 in. x 3 in. and stick with tape. Tape it onto the lid to make a funnel.

Ahoy there!

Try out your boats in water to see if they float or sink. If you blow against the sails, do they move?

What next?

Try putting some objects in your boat make it heavier. Do it still float?

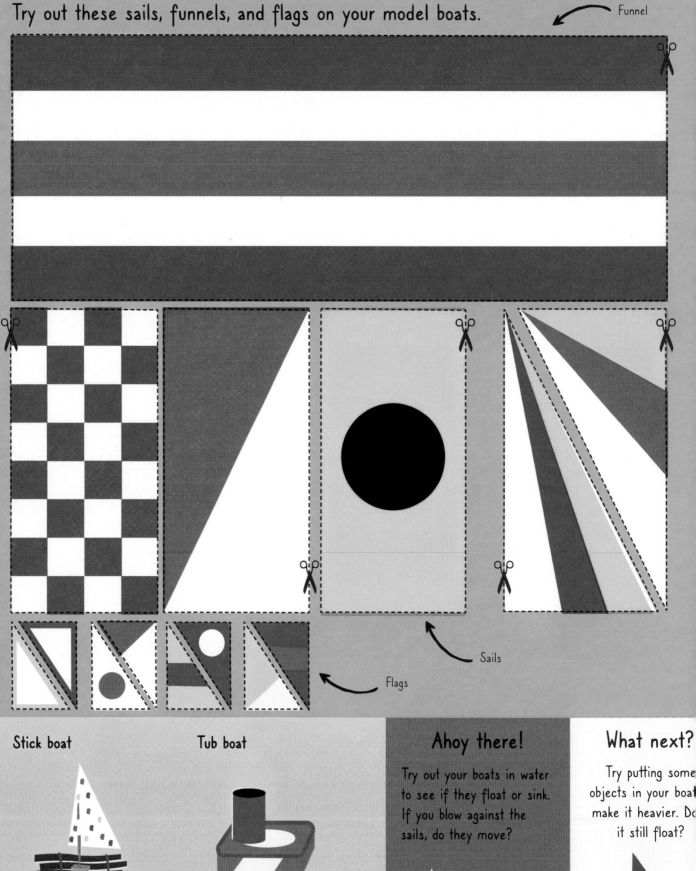

PASS ON A SECRET
using chemical reactions

Invisible ink has been used for centuries to deliver hidden messages. The letters only appear if you know how to reveal them.

Lemon juice works well as invisible ink because it has very little color on paper. But when heated, the juice turns brown.

Invisible ink

secret

You will need

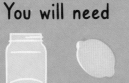

jar

lemon

pen

paintbrushes

spoon

paper

blow-dryer

1 Ask an adult to cut a lemon in half. Squeeze the juice into a jar.

2 Add a few drops of water and mix the solution with a spoon.

Where is the best place in this scene to hide a secret message? Mark it with a lemon juice cross.

ICE CREAM PARLOR

Can a friend guess your hiding place? Reveal it to them with a hair dryer.

FRESH FRUIT

Meet me at 3 o'clock

With a pen, write a short message on the top half of a piece of paper.

Meet me at 3 o'clock

at the ice cream parlor

Now, use a paintbrush dipped in the lemon to write a secret message below.

Meet me at 3 o'clock

at the ice cream parlor

To reveal the secret message, use a blow-dryer to heat up the paper. Ask an adult to help you.

What's happening?

When lemon juice is heated, a chemical reaction takes place. The juice turns brown and the message is revealed.

What next?

Do any other foods work as invisible ink?

Try milk, apple juice or vinegar.

EXPLORE WHEELS
by making a spinning machine

21

Use a wheel to make a bubble machine.

A wheel is a simple machine. It makes the work of moving objects much easier.

It's faster to go on roller skates than it is to walk!

Wheels are always circular because this is the best shape for fast and smooth movement.

Bubble wheel

You will need

circle template (7 in. diameter)

corrugated card

compass

pen

2 cardboard paper towel tubes

2 bamboo skewers

a dish of bubble mixture

tape

scissors

4 pipe cleaners

1 Set your compass to 3 1/2 in. and draw a 7-in.-wide circle onto corrugated card.

2 Cut the circle out and push two skewers through the center. Tape both ends.

Trace around this template
to make your corrugated
card bubble wheel.

Or cut it out and
stick it on your
wheel as decoratio

What next?

What happens if yo
make a square-shap
bubble wand?

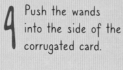

3 Make 4 bubble wands. Form a loop in a pipe cleaner and twist the ends to secure it.

4 Push the wands into the side of the corrugated card.

5 Cut slits into the tubes. The wheel will need to reach the mixture.

6 Spin the wheel so each wand collects bubble mixture, and blow as you spin!

USE ELASTIC ENERGY
to send an object flying

If you pull a rubber band, it stretches. When you let it go, it springs back. This stored, or potential, energy can be used to fling objects through the air.

This machine uses potential energy to fling the balls over the castle walls.

Plane launcher

You will need

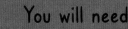

card 8 in. x 8 in. or template

stapler

Medium rubber band

paper planes (see instructions on the inside back cover)

1 Fold the card in half. With the crease along the top, fold one side back up to the crease.

2 Fold the other side up to the crease.

Fold the lines to make the plane launcher.

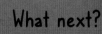

What next?

Try out different paper plane designs.

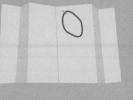

3 Now fold each side flap down in half again.

4 Open up the card and staple a rubber band at one end of the center crease.

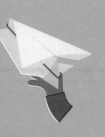

5 Close up the card with the centerfold at the bottom and the double-fold at the top. Pull the rubber band over the top.

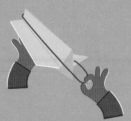

6 Place the plane in the slot at the top. Pull the flaps apart to launch!

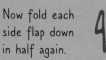

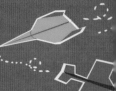

How far can you make them zoom?

INVENT A MAZE
to challenge your marble skills

Mazes have been confusing people for centuries! Hedge mazes were invented for having fun. They were also used to hide in for secret meetings.

Mazes can be built using walls, hedges, or even crops such as corn.

Maze

You will need

large square of card or template on the next page.

ruler

pen

scissors

marble

glue stick

thin card

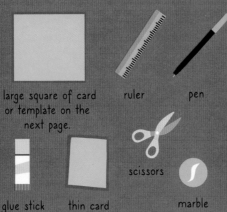

1. Make a fold line 1.2 in. in from the edges of the card. Snip along one edge of each corner.

glue

glue

glue

glue

glue

2. Fold up the sides of the box and glue the flaps to keep them in place.

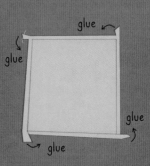

Use this base for your maze.

What next?

Use other material to make walls for your maze. Try straws, sponges, or clay!

maze wall

curved maze wall

 **3** Cut a piece of card 4 in. x 1 in.. Fold it in half, unfold, and snip three times up to the fold.

 **4** Fold the flaps so the wall stands up. Glue the flaps and position on your maze.

 5 Cut a piece of card 4 in. x 1 in.. Fold in half, unfold, and snip up every 1/2 in.. Fold the wall up and bend it to shape.

6 Make lots of walls. Stick them into place to make a path. Pop in a marble and tip the maze to make it run!

SLOW A FALL
with air resistance

Gravity is the invisible force that pulls everything down to Earth.

Air resistance is a kind of friction that slows down the movement of objects through the air.

Parachutes let things fall from a height slowly and land safely. When a parachute opens, the air resistance increases, slowing the fall down.

Parachute

You will need

card or paper, about 8 in. x 8 in. or template

4 x 20 in. pieces of string

ruler

scissors

tape

small toy

1 Measure 1 in. down two opposite sides of the card or paper. Draw guidelines.

2 Fold each side in along the lines.

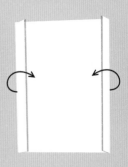

Use this template to make a parachute.

Fold along the dotted white lines.

Fold along the dotted white lines.

What next?

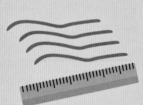

3 Cut four pieces of string, each about 20 in. long.

4 Attach one piece of string to each corner with tape.

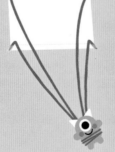

5 Tie the ends of the string to your toy.

Can you drop an egg i cup without it breakin

USE WIND ENERGY
and fly a kite

Today, people fly kites for fun. But hundreds of years ago, kites were invented by Chinese soldiers to measure distances and to send messages.

Wind energy makes the kite move and dance.

A tail helps the kite to balance so it flies more steadily.

The string stops the kite from flying away!

Kite

You will need

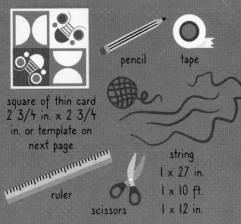

square of thin card 2 3/4 in. x 2 3/4 in. or template on next page

pencil

tape

string
1 x 27 in.
1 x 10 ft.
1 x 12 in.

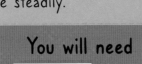
ruler

scissors

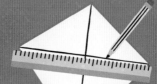

1 Lay the card flat. Use a ruler to draw diagonal lines from corner to corner.

2 Fold three corners into the middle. Cut the fourth corner off and keep to one side.

Use this template to make your own kite.

Fold along the white dotted lines.

Fold along the white dotted lines.

What next?

Fly your kite. Try making a bigger kite with longer string.

3 Tie a knot on each end of the 27 in. string. Attach to two corners with tape.

4 Find the center of the string and attach the 10 ft. string to it with a knot.

5 Use the corner you cut off to make lots of small triangles.

6 Tape the small triangles along the 12 in. piece of string, and tape to the kite.

BUILD 3D DICE

and invent a new game

26

Use nets to make different-shaped dice.

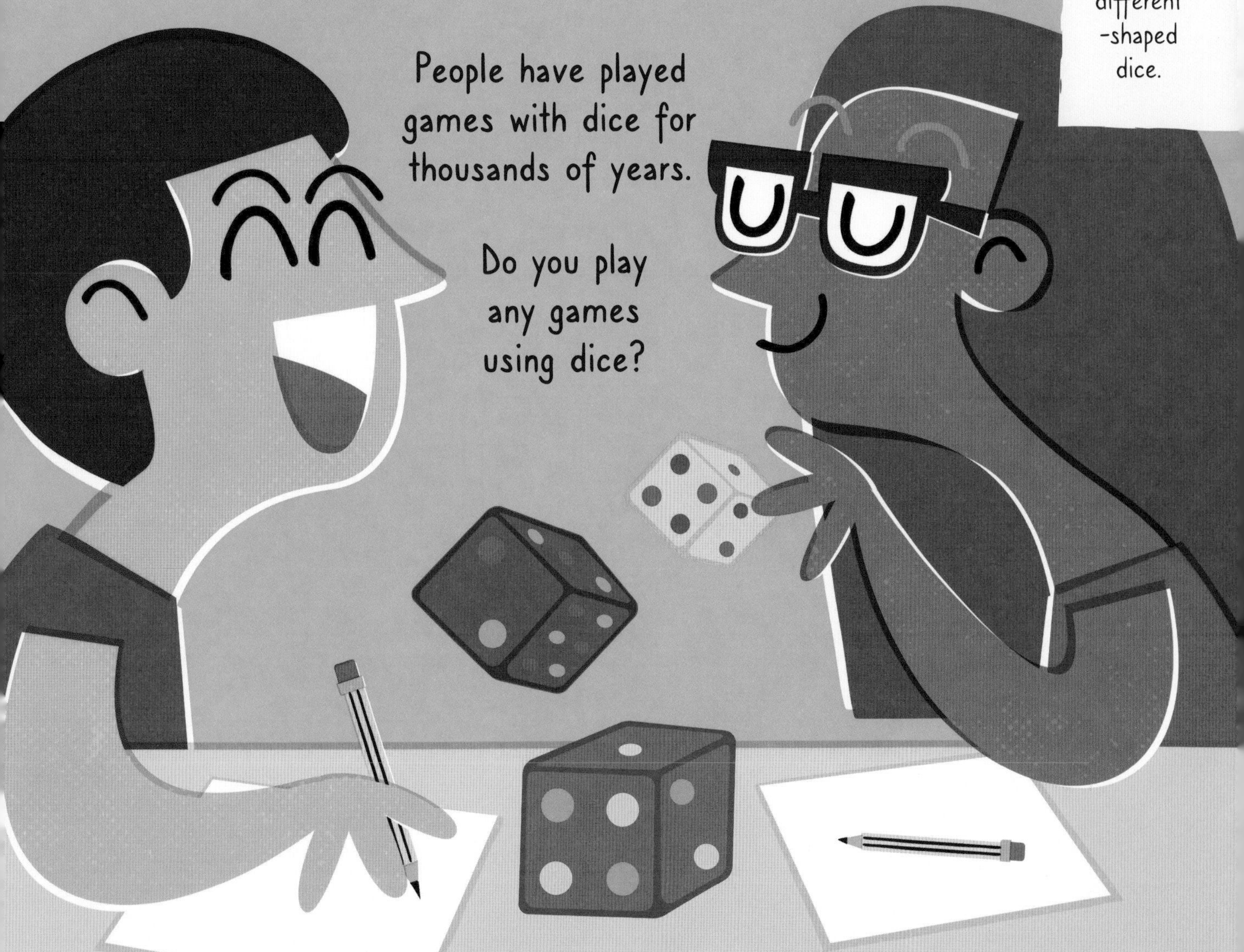

People have played games with dice for thousands of years.

Do you play any games using dice?

Turn over to find out how to play the dice game ***One and Done***. Can you invent your own dice game?

6-sided dice

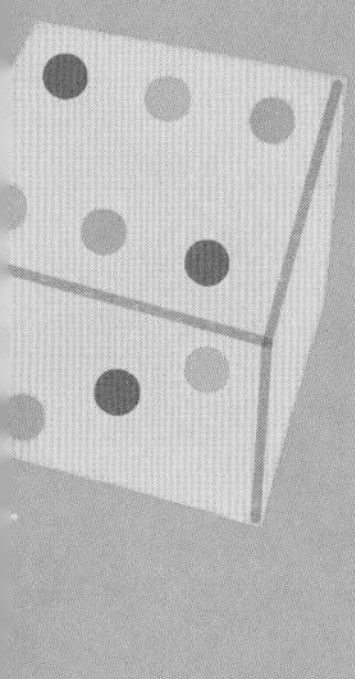

You will need

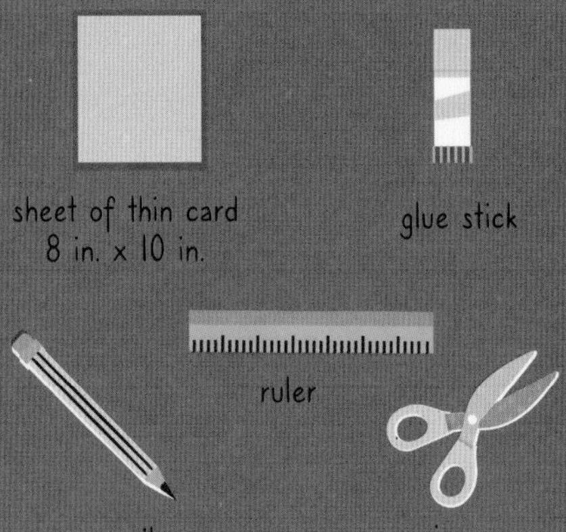

sheet of thin card
8 in. x 10 in.
glue stick
ruler
pencil
scissors

1 Draw a 1 1/2 in. x 1 1/2 in. square on a piece of card.

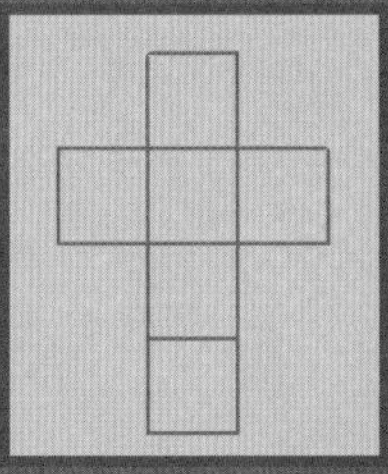

2 Draw five more squares, the same size, to make this shape.

Dice can have more than six sides. Trace this net, fold the lines, glue the tabs, and fold it into an 8-sided dice.

An 8-sided dice is called an octahedron.

Nets are patterns that can be folded up to create 3D shapes.

2

6

5

7

3

9

1

8

You will need

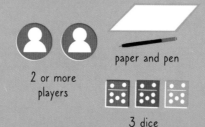

2 or more players

paper and pen

3 dice

How to play 'One and Done'

1 The oldest starts and rolls the dice.

2 If a 1 is rolled, the person is out and play moves to the next person.

3 If player doesn't get a 1, write down the scores and add them up.

4 First player to 75 wins!

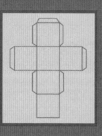

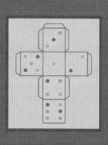

3 Add 1/2 in. tabs to the sides of four of the squares to complete the net.

4 Draw dots, from one to six, in each square.

5 Cut around the outside of the net and fold along each line.

6 Glue each tab and fold up into a cube, using the tabs to hold it in place.

What next?

Can you make a 12-sided dice?

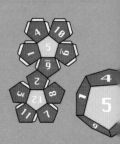

EXPLORE FRICTION
with rolling wheels

27

Make a speedy downhill racer.

Wheels are an amazing invention. They make easy work of dragging a heavy object over a bumpy surface.

Gravity is the force that pulls things downward.

Friction is a force that acts in the opposite direction to a moving object, slowing it down.

Gravity pulls a vehicle down a hill fast, while friction slows it down.

Wheels help a vehicle to overcome friction so it can travel faster.

Downhill racer

You will need

4 x plastic bottle tops

2 x toothpicks

clothespin

tape

coloring pens

scissors

card or templates

large box or cardboard for track

straw

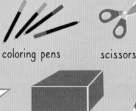

1 Ask an adult to make a hole in the center of each bottle top with a toothpick.

2 Cut two 1 in. lengths from the straw. Push them onto each toothpick.

Try out these racer templates.

What next?

Make a racer wit[h] bigger wheels. Is [it] better at beating friction?

3 Attach the wheels to the toothpicks.

4 Grip one set of wheels to the clothespin, and push the other firmly onto the back.

5 Use the templates above to design a vehicle on card. Fold it and tape it to the clothespin.

6 Make a racing slope out of an old piece of cardboard. Get set, GO!

RECORD THE WEATHER
using a weather vane

Wind vanes were invented to show the direction the wind is blowing.

A spinning arrow points in the direction the wind is coming from—north, south, east, or west.

People in hot air balloons use wind vanes to check where they will travel.

Weather vane

You will need

Thin card or template on next page

scissors

pencil

glue stick

2 card rectangles
6 in. x 1 in. or template

tape   sticky tack

1 Roll the large card rectangle loosely around a pencil. Fix with tape.

2 Squeeze one end of the tube and use tape to seal it closed.

Cut along the
dotted black
lines to use
these templates.

How to find north

A compass shows north, south, east, and
west. The moving needle of a compass
always points to the north.

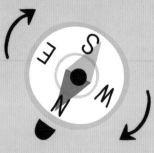

Twist the compass around until
the pointer lines up to the N. The
direction it is pointing to is north.

When you make the cross,
make sure the N, S, E, and W
are in the correct positions.

W

E

N

S

What next?

Make sure your N
pointer faces north.
it spin in the wind
find out which direct
the wind is blowing

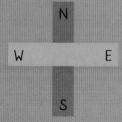

Glue the card pieces
in a cross. Mark N,
E, S, and W exactly
as shown.

Place the sticky tack
in the center of the
cross and stand a
pencil in it.

Design and cut out
a character holding
an arrow, or use the
template above.

Attach the tube to the
cutout with tape. Slide
the tube onto the
pencil. Take it outside.

TEST A PENDULUM
by making a demolition ball

Pendulums are swinging weights. They are used in clocks and make the tick-tock sound as they swing back and forth, keeping time.

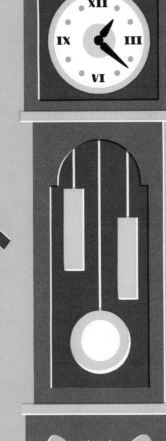

A weight will swing more quickly if the pendulum is short.

A weight will swing more slowly if it is long.

Demolition ball

You will need

4 strips of card 1/2 in. x 8 in. or strips on the next page

1 strip of card 1/2 in. x 4 in. or template

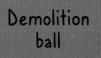
tangerine or small orange

string

tape

1 Take one long strip of card and wrap it around the orange to form a loop. Fix with tape.

2 Tape the other long strips one at a time, making sure the loops all overlap at the top.

Heavy steel demolition balls hang from huge cranes on cables or chains. These powerful pendulums demolish buildings as they swing back and forth.

Cut out these strips to make your own demolition ball.

Place the short strip of card under the top loop. Curl up and tape the ends together to make a ring.

Tie one end of the string to the small ring and the other end to a washing line.

Build towers from blocks or old boxes. Can you get your demolition ball to knock down your tower?

What next?

Try the demolition ball pendulum with a longer or shorter string. Time the swings.

What happe

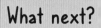

LIFT OFF INTO SPACE
by making a rocket

30
Launch a rocket high up into the sky.

It takes hundreds of inventors and engineers to send people into Space! The aerodynamic shape of a rocket helps it to cut through the air like a knife.

The force that pushes a rocket upward is called thrust.

Rockets have very powerful jet engines to push them off the ground and away from Earth's gravity.

Rocket

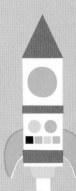

You will need

6 in. x 2 in. card strip

6 in. x 3 in. card or rockets on next page

glue stick

paper straw

pencil

tape

1 Wrap the card strip around a pencil to make a tube. Tape in place. Remove the pencil.

2 Squash the end of the tube flat and seal it up completely with tape.

Try using these different rockets.

Which rocket do you like the best?

Does one rocket go farther than the rest?

What next?

Try blowing in differe ways—soft, hard, slo quick. Does it mak a difference?

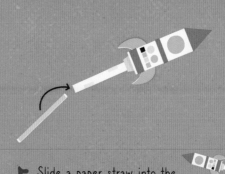

3 Draw, color in, and cut out a rocket from card. Or use one of the rockets above.

4 Stick the rocket onto the flat end of the tube with glue.

5 Slide a paper straw into the end of the tube and blow! How far does your rocket go?